Cover and Title pages: Nathan Love

www.mheonline.com/readingwonders

Send all inquiries to:
McGraw-Hill Education
2 Penn Plaza
New York, NY 10121

ISBN: 978-0-07-680007-0
MHID: 0-07-680007-5

Printed in the United States of America.

6 7 8 9 LWI 20 19 18

C

Wonders

Program Authors

Diane August

Donald R. Bear

Janice A. Dole

Jana Echevarria

Douglas Fisher

David Francis

Vicki Gibson

Jan Hasbrouck

Margaret Kilgo

Jay McTighe

Scott G. Paris

Timothy Shanahan

Josefina V. Tinajero

Mc
Graw
Hill
Education

Unit 2

Our Community

The Big Idea
What makes a community?　　6

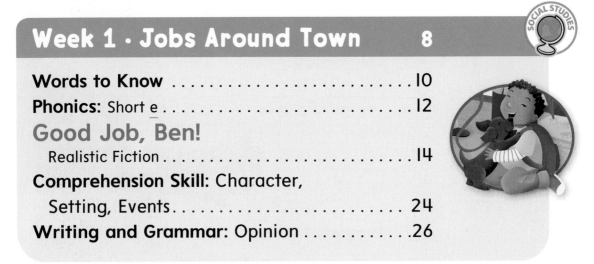
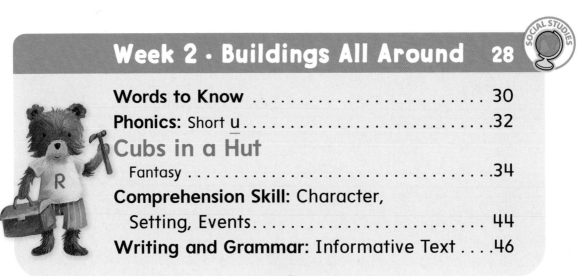
SOCIAL STUDIES

SOCIAL STUDIES

(t) Diane Greenseid; (c) Robin Boyer; (b) Amanda Gulliver

4

Unit 2
Our Community

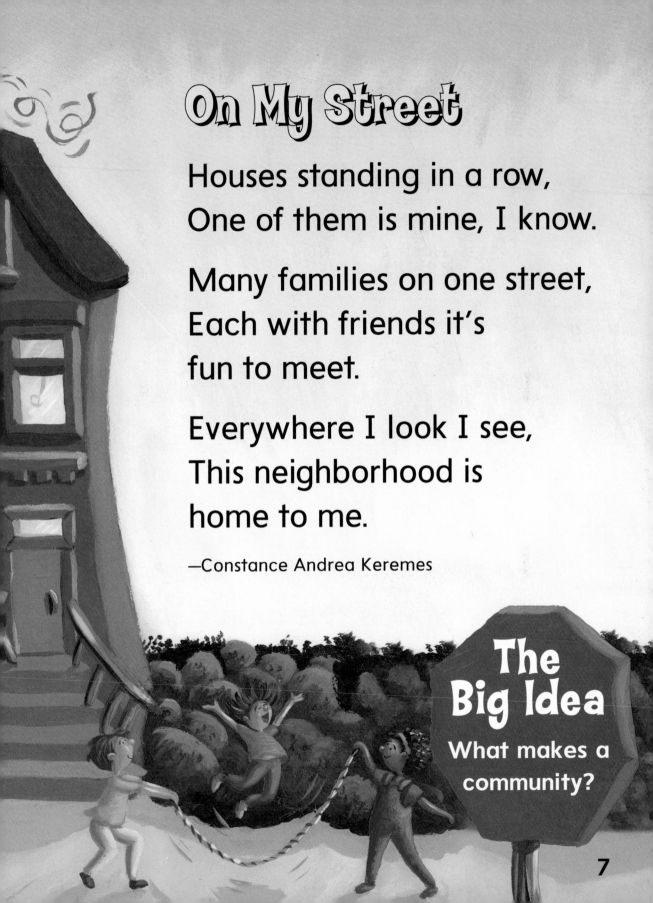

On My Street

Houses standing in a row,
One of them is mine, I know.

Many families on one street,
Each with friends it's
fun to meet.

Everywhere I look I see,
This neighborhood is
home to me.

—Constance Andrea Keremes

The Big Idea

What makes a
community?

Essential Question

What jobs need to be done in a community?

Go Digital!

At Work

Talk About It

How is this man's work important in the community?

again

I may need to bake it **again.**

help

She will **help** find the street.

new

My class has a **new** teacher.

there

There is a lot of mail in his bag.

use

Use a scoop to pick up the rocks.

COLLABORATE

Your Turn

Say the sentence for each word. Then make up another sentence.

Go Digital! *Use the online visual glossary*

(tl) Bananastock/Alamy; (cl) Masterfile; (bl) Corbis; (tr) Design Pics Inc./Alamy; (br) Steve Allen/Brand X Pictures/Getty Images

Short e

The letters e or ea can make the short e sound, as in **get** or **bread**.

men	vet	pet
bed	red	mess
head	well	dress
smell	deaf	bread

Fr<u>e</u>d's p<u>e</u>t h<u>e</u>n can p<u>e</u>ck!

The top of its h<u>ea</u>d is r<u>e</u>d.

Your Turn

COLLABORATE

Look for these words with the short <u>e</u> sound in "Good Job, Ben!"

B<u>e</u>n	h<u>ea</u>d	g<u>e</u>t	y<u>e</u>t
m<u>e</u>n	w<u>e</u>t	st<u>e</u>p	br<u>ea</u>d
sm<u>e</u>lls	t<u>e</u>n	J<u>e</u>t	v<u>e</u>t
w<u>e</u>ll	p<u>e</u>t	Gl<u>e</u>nn	r<u>ea</u>d

13

Essential Question

What jobs need to be done in a community?

Read about jobs that people do around town.

Go Digital!

Robin Boyer

14

Good Job, Ben!

Ben and Mom head to town.
It is a big trip.
There is a lot to see.

Ben and Mom will get on the bus.
The driver stops on this block.

Good job!

Ben and Mom can not cross yet.
Stop! Stop! She can **help** them.

Big job!

Ben and Mom walk past.
Six men **use** a drill and fill cracks.
It will look **new again**.

Wet job!

19

Ben and Mom step in for bread.

Ben sniffs. It smells good.

Mom gets ten.

Hot job!

Ben and Mom get Jet.

Jet licks Ben.

The vet helped Jet get well quick.

Pet job!

Ben and Mom stop for books.
Ben can get help from Miss Glenn.

Glad job!

What did Ben get?
What has he read?
Ben read books on jobs.

Good job, Ben!

Character, Setting, Events

A **character** is a person or animal in a story.

The **setting** is where a story takes place.

The **events** are what happen in a story.

 Find Text Evidence

Find the characters, the setting, and an event.

page 16

Ben and Mom head to town.
It is a big trip.
There is a lot to see.

Characters	Setting	Events
Ben Mom	at the bus stop	They are going to town.
Ben Mom	bakery	They buy bread.
Ben Mom	library	Ben finds books about jobs.

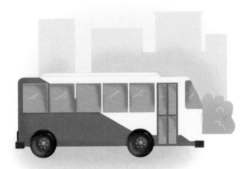

Your Turn

COLLABORATE

Talk about other characters, settings, and events in "Good Job, Ben!"

Go Digital! Use the interactive graphic organizer

25

Write About the Text

Pages 14–23

Eva

Focus on an Idea
I wrote about the men's hats.

Clues
I used the picture to figure out a reason for my opinion.

I answered the question: **Which hat in "Good Job, Ben!" do you think is the best for the worker's job?**

Student Model: *Opinion*

I think the six men's hats are the best for their job.

The men fix the street.

They wear hard, yellow hats.

Hard hats keep the men safe.

They guard the men's heads.

The hard hats are the best.

Grammar

Hats is an example of a **noun**.

Your Turn

Which job in "Good Job, Ben!" would you like to have? Why? Use text evidence to support your answer.

Go Digital!
Write your response online.
Use your editing checklist.

27

Essential Question

What buildings do you know?
What are they made of?

Go Digital!

Sakis Papadopoulos/robertharding/Getty Images

Our Town

COLLABORATE

Talk About It

What kinds of buildings are in this city?

could

They **could** build a house with logs.

live

Do you **live** in a tall building?

one

This hut has **one** room.

then

We open the door, and **then** we go out.

three

Three people can fit in a tent.

Your Turn

Say the sentence for each word. Then make up another sentence.

Go Digital! *Use the online visual glossary*

Short u

The letter u can make the short u sound in **hut**.

up	fun	but
bus	cup	duck
bug	drum	mud
tub	tucked	stuff

Buzz the bug can live in mud.

But can Buzz run and have fun?

Your Turn

COLLABORATE

Look for these words with short u in "Cubs in a Hut."

cubs	hut	Gus	mud
Russ	fun	Bud	up
rugs	stuff	us	snug
bugs	rug		

Essential Question

What buildings do you know? What are they made of?

Read about how three cubs build a hut.

Go Digital!

Amanda Gulliver

34

"Let's make a hut," said Gus.

"We **could** use mud," said Russ.

"It will be fun!" said Bud.

Amanda Gulliver

36

The cubs had a plan.
Bud got a big stack of sticks.
Russ and Gus got mud
and grass.

The cubs did a very good job.

"Let's move in!" yelled Russ.

"Yes, yes!" yelled Bud and Gus.

The cubs set up rugs and beds.
They filled up the hut with lots
of stuff.

Then **one** night **three** cubs got up.

Drip, drip, drip!

"My bed is wet!" yelled Bud.

"My head is wet!" yelled Gus.

"It's not fun to **live** in a wet hut!" yelled Russ.

"We must fix it," said Bud.

"It will not drip on us," said Gus.

"We will not get wet," said Russ.

It is good to live in a dry hut.
Three cubs are as snug as bugs
in a rug!

Character, Setting, Events

A character is a person or animal in a story.

The setting is where a story takes place.

The events are what happen in a story.

 Find Text Evidence

Use the words and the pictures to find a character, setting, and event in the story.

page 37

The cubs had a plan.
Bud got a big stack of sticks.
Russ and Gus got mud
and grass.

Amanda Gulliver

Character	Setting	Events
Bud	forest	He got sticks.
Russ	forest	He got mud.
Gus	forest	He got grass.

COLLABORATE

Your Turn

Talk about the characters, setting, and events in "Cubs in a Hut."

Go Digital! *Use the interactive graphic organizer*

45

Write About the Text

Pages 34–43

Luis

I responded to the prompt: **What do the cubs do first, next, and last to fix the roof of their hut?**

Student Model: *Informative Text*

The cubs must fix the roof.

First, the cubs get nails.

Then, they get wood.

Next, they find a ladder.

Beginning Sentence

I wrote a beginning that names the topic.

Clues

I used the picture to figure out what the cubs do.

Then, they go up to the roof.
Last, they pound the nails.
Now the roof is fixed!

Grammar

The **singular noun** and **plural noun** are used correctly.

Your Turn

COLLABORATE

Look at pages 36 through 39. What plans did the bears use for building their hut? Write the directions they followed. Use details from the story in your answer.

Go Digital!
Write your response online.
Use your editing checklist.

Amanda Gulliver

47

Essential Question

Where do animals live together?

Go Digital!

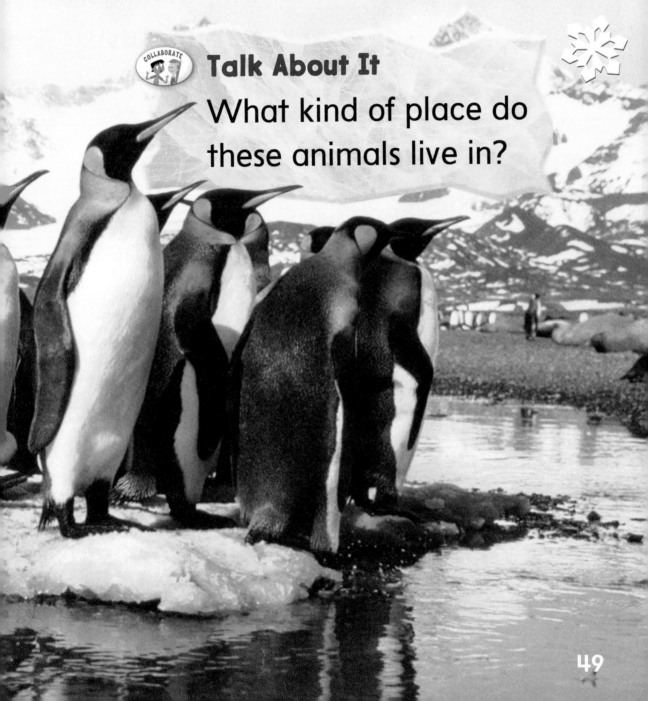

Animals at Home

Talk About It

What kind of place do these animals live in?

eat

Chipmunks like to **eat** nuts.

no

A snake has **no** legs.

of

The birds sit in a nest **of** twigs.

under

They dive down **under** the water.

who

Who can see the bug?

Your Turn

COLLABORATE

Say the sentence for each word. Then make up another sentence.

Go Digital! *Use the online visual glossary*

End Blends

The letters nd, nk, nt, sk, st, and mp together make the ending sounds in **land**, **drink**, **went**, **ask**, **rest**, and **damp**.

a**nd**	fa**st**	ju**mp**
se**nd**	de**sk**	mu**st**
hu**nt**	ma**sk**	pla**nt**
sku**nk**	tru**nk**	sta**mp**

The skunk is plump and fast!

It will play and hunt.

Your Turn
COLLABORATE

Look for these words with end blends in "The Best Spot."

best	plants	nest
trunk	ants	and
rest	sand	stump
jump	must	hunts
dusk	went	skunk

Essential Question

Where do animals live together?

Read about the animals in a forest.

Go Digital!

The Best Spot

(t to b) Dave Cole/Alamy; Gail Shumway/Photographer's Choice/Getty Images

This is a forest.

This spot has lots **of** animals.

Deer live here. They **eat** plants.

But **who** is in the grass?

A rabbit's head pops up!

What is up there?

Look up, up, up.

It is a nest.

The mom gets big bugs. Yum!

What is on the trunk?

It is a nest, too.

Lots of wasps live in it.

(t to b) Philippe Clement/Nature Picture Library; IT Stock Free/Alamy

Ants live here, too.

Ants pick up twigs and grass.

Ants zip in and out.

Ants have **no** rest!

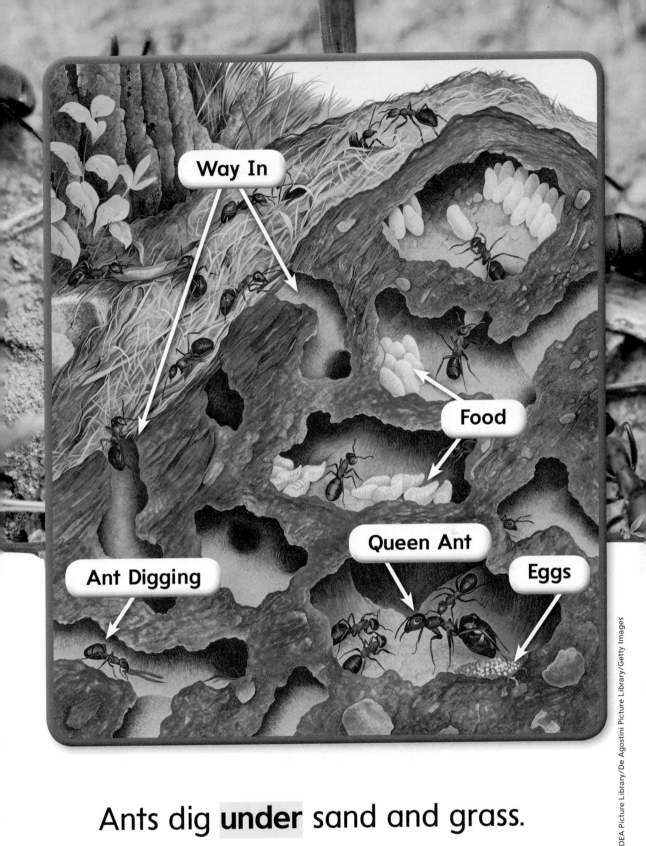

Way In

Food

Ant Digging

Queen Ant

Eggs

Ants dig **under** sand and grass.

Fox kits hop on a stump.

Mom fox lets the kits run and jump.

The kits must eat.

Dad fox hunts at dusk.

Who went hunting, too?
A skunk!

This spot has lots of animals!

Main Topic and Key Details

The **main topic** is what the selection is about.

Key details give information about the main topic.

 Find Text Evidence

The selection is about a place where animals live together.

Find a detail about one of the animals.

page 56

This is a forest.

This spot has lots **of** animals.

Deer live here. They **eat** plants.

Main Topic		
Lots of animals live in the forest.		
Detail	**Detail**	**Detail**
Deer live in the forest. They eat plants.	Ants make their home under the ground.	Some forest animals hunt at night.

Your Turn

Talk about the main topic and other details in "The Best Spot."

Go Digital! Use the interactive graphic organizer

Write About the Text

Pages 54–63

Ben

I responded to the prompt: **Write two pages of an informative text about animals that live in the sea.**

Student Model: *Informative Text*

This is a sea.

This spot has lots of animals.

Sharks live here.

Main Idea

My first two sentences are about my main idea.

Facts

I included facts to tell about the sea.

Alexandra Pavlova/Moment Open/Getty Images

66

Sharks eat fish.

But who is behind a rock?

A turtle's head pops out!

Grammar

Possessive nouns tell who or what has or owns something. **Turtle's** is a possessive noun.

Your Turn

COLLABORATE

Use "The Best Spot" as a model and write the first two pages of an informative text about animals that live in a park.

Go Digital!
Write your response online.
Use your editing checklist.

Universal Stopping Point Photography/Flickr/Getty Images

Essential Question

How do people help out in the community?

Go Digital!

Make It Better

Talk About It

What are these children doing together to make a difference?

all

Let's pick up **all** the trash.

call

Who will you **call** to help?

day

It is a good **day** to plant.

her

Mom recycles **her** bottles.

want

I **want** to help my Gram.

Your Turn

COLLABORATE

Say the sentence for each word. Then make up another sentence.

Go Digital! *Use the online visual glossary*

(tl) Leland BobbÉ/Corbis; (cl) STOCK4B GmbH/Alamy; (bl) Maria Spann/Photographer's Choice/Getty Images; (tr) Image Source/Alamy (br) Hill Street Studios/Blend Images/Getty Images

<u>th</u>, <u>sh</u>, -<u>ng</u>

The letters th make the sound you hear in **that** or **path**.

The letters sh make the sound you hear in **shop** or **fish**.

The letters -ng make the sound you hear in **ring**.

then	**shut**	**wing**
math	**thank**	**hang**
shed	**sing**	**crash**
with	**fresh**	**sting**

Sergio DeGiorgi

I bang my drum on this ship.

Can Beth sing a song?

Your Turn

Look for these words with th, sh, and -ng in "Thump Thump Helps Out."

thump	thumped	sang	
hush	that	bang	
crash	wish	Sheldon	
think	rushed	long	
with	song	brings	this

Thump Thump liked to thump.

He thumped a lot as he sang.

He thumped a lot just for fun.

"Hush! Stop that, Thump Thump!"
yelled **all** the little rabbits.

"We do not like it one bit!"

But Thump Thump did not stop.

One **day**, there was a problem.

Thump Thump's bus hit a rock.

Bang! Crash! Clunk!

His bus got stuck in the mud.

The little rabbits could not fix it.

Sergio DeGiorgi

78

"We wish big rabbits could get us home," sniffed the little rabbits.

"Help us!" yelled Miss Sheldon.

But not one big rabbit heard **her call**.

Thump Thump had a plan.

"I think I can help," he sang.

He thumped and thumped and thumped.

Big rabbits all over heard
Thump Thump's thump.

They rushed to help fix the bus.

The kids got home fast.

"Thump Thump, can you help us?" asked the big rabbits.

"We **want** you to thump loud and long if a rabbit needs help."

"Thump, Thump!" went Thump
Thump, with a song.

And Thump Thump thumps and
brings help to this day.

Character, Setting, Events

A **character** is a person or animal in a story.

The **setting** is where a story takes place.

The **events** are what happen in a story.

 Find Text Evidence

Use the words and pictures to find the events that happen in the story.

page 76

Thump Thump liked to thump.

He thumped a lot as he sang.

He thumped a lot just for fun.

Sergio DeGiorgi

Characters	Setting	Events
Thump Thump	forest	He thumped his feet a lot.
Rabbits	forest	The bus hit a rock and got stuck in the mud.
Thump Thump	forest	He thumped his feet to get help.

Your Turn

COLLABORATE

Talk about the characters, setting, and events in "Thump Thump Helps Out."

Go Digital! Use the interactive graphic organizer

Pages 74–83

Write About the Text

Robert

I responded to the prompt: **Write a fantasy about a helpful character. Use "Thump Thump" as a model.**

Student Model: *Narrative Text*

Beginning
My story has a beginning.

Chip Chipmunk likes to run.

He runs up and down trees.

He runs quickly in the park.

One day Chip passes Dad.

Chip's Grandma is sick.

Chip's Dad has nuts for her.

Grammar

A **proper noun,** such as **Chip,** begins with a capital letter.

"Could I help you, Dad?"

Chip asks.

"I can run the nuts to Grandma's house."

Chip is so helpful!

Characters
I made the animals talk like in the story.

Your Turn

Use "Thump Thump Helps Out" as a model to write a fantasy about a character who has an unusual habit.

Go Digital!
Write your response online.
Use your editing checklist.

Essential Question

How can you find your way around?

Go Digital!

Map It!

COLLABORATE

Talk About It

What is the family using
to get directions?

89

around

I like to ride **around** the park.

by

The bus stops **by** my house.

many

There are **many** shops in town.

place

Let's look for this **place** on a map.

walk

We **walk** to the library.

COLLABORATE

Your Turn

Say the sentence for each word.
Then make up another sentence.

Go Digital! *Use the online visual glossary*

<u>ch</u>, -<u>tch</u>, <u>wh</u>, <u>ph</u>

The letters ch and -tch make the sound you hear in **chop** and **catch**.

The letters wh make the sound you hear in **when**.

The letters ph make the sound you hear in **Phil**.

inch	whiz	chat
itch	when	graph
lunch	check	stitch
which	sketch	much

Phil will sketch a graph for math.

When will he get his lunch?

Your Turn

Look for these words with ch, -tch, wh, and ph in "Which Way on the Map?"

which	Mitch	Steph
children	chat	benches
catch	such	lunch check

Genre Nonfiction

Essential Question
How can you find your way around?

Read about places in a town.

Go Digital!

Which Way on the Map?

Mitch and Steph live in a big town.

There is a lot to see.

Let's **walk around** with them.

This is the town on a map.

It shows each **place** in town.

This place has red bricks.

Many children go here.

Mitch and Steph go here, too.

Which place is this?

Can you spot it on the map?

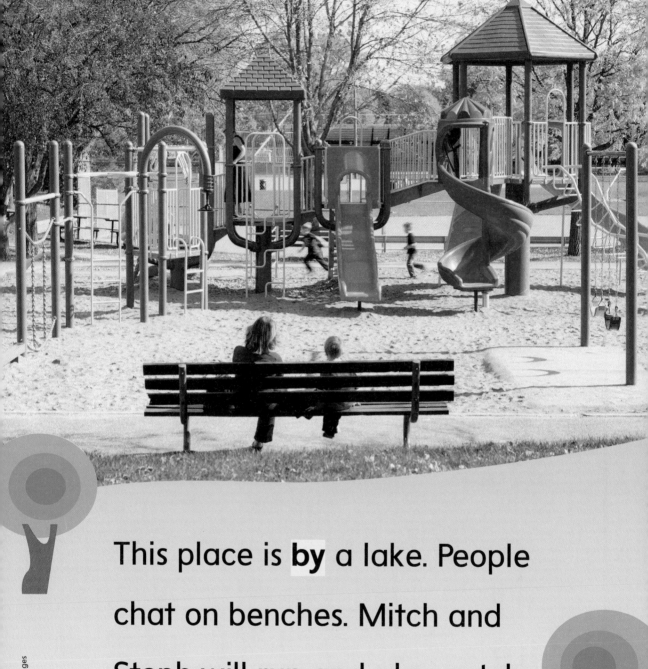

This place is **by** a lake. People

chat on benches. Mitch and

Steph will run and play catch.

It is such fun!

Which place is this?

Can you spot it on the map?

This place has a big box. Mitch and Steph stop and get stamps. They drop a letter in the big box. Which place is this?

Can you spot it on the map?

Where can Mitch and Steph get lunch?

Check the map!

Main Topic and Key Details

The **main topic** is what the selection is about.

Key details give information about the main topic.

🔍 Find Text Evidence

The selection is about how to use a map.

Find a detail about the school in Mitch and Steph's town.

page 98

This place has red bricks.

Main Topic
How to Use a Map to Find Places in Town

Detail	Detail	Detail
The school has red bricks. The school is on the map.	The playground is by the lake. The playground is on the map.	The post office has a big box. The post office is on the map.

Your Turn

COLLABORATE

Talk about the main topic and details in "Which Way on the Map?"

Go Digital! *Use the interactive graphic organizer*

Pages 94–103

Write About the Text

Maria

Clues

I used pictures from the maps to help me answer the question.

I answered the question: **Which of the map features help Mitch and Steph get around town?**

Student Model: *Informative Text*

The pictures and signs on the map help Mitch and Steph. Mitch and Steph look at the pictures on the map. The pictures look like places in town.

Tetra Images/Getty Images

106

Supporting Details
I included details about signs.

The signs tell them the names of the places.
The children can tell where they are using the pictures and words.

Grammar
The word **children** is an **irregular plural noun.** It means more than one child.

COLLABORATE

Your Turn

Why does the author use photographs and parts of the map? What does this help a reader to understand? Use text evidence to support your answer.

Go Digital!
Write your response online.
Use your editing checklist.

DAJ/Getty Images